PLANT CARE

RP MINIS

PHILADELPHIA

RP Minis®
Hachette Book Group
1290 Avenue of the Americas, New York, NY 10104
www.runningpress.com
@Running_Press

First edition: April 2023

Published by RP Minis, an imprint of Perseus Books, LLC, a
subsidiary of Hachette Book Group, Inc. The RP Minis name
and logo is a registered trademark of the Hachette Book Group.

The Hachette Speakers Bureau provides a wide range of
authors for speaking events. To find out more, go to
www.hachettespeakersbureau.com or call (866) 376-6591.

The publisher is not responsible for websites (or their content)
that are not owned by the publisher.

ISBN: 978-0-7624-8228-3

Contents

YOU HAVE A PLANT, NOW WHAT?

"My green thumb came
only as a result of the
mistakes I made while
learning to see things from
the plant's point of view."

—H. FRED DALE

Plants can't talk, so how could you possibly know what they want? Don't worry: It's not rocket science! While every plant baby will have its own unique needs, there are aspects of care and maintenance that will hold true for many indoor and outdoor varieties, and understanding the basics will help you be the most responsible plant parent possible.

Consider this mini book your primer on plant care 101. We'll start with the key ingredients necessary to keep a plant alive, then progress into more advanced aspects of care, like maintenance, troubleshooting common issues, and specific tips by plant type.

PLANT CARE 101: BASIC PLANT NEEDS

First things's first: All plants need light, oxygen, and water to survive. (We'll get to soil in a bit.)

This holy trinity of ingredients make up the recipe for photosynthesis, a process where plants convert light, oxygen, and water into energy. Without it, plants can't bloom, grow, or produce seeds.

Oxygen is taken care of—it's all around us. If it's not, you probably have much bigger problems than keeping plants alive. Light and water will require a bit more effort on your part. Different plants will have different needs for each of these. Not sure what those needs are? In general, you'll

want to consider a plant's native
environment for clues about
its proper care. For instance,
a plant that comes from the
desert might need a lot of light
but not that much water, but a
plant from the rain forest might
crave high humidity and warm
temperatures.

Here are some general tips
about providing your plants with
light and water.

Light

What happens if a plant gets no light? The short answer is that it will die of starvation. Without light, a plant can't create chlorophyll, the compound that gives plants color and helps them absorb energy through the sun. Even if a plant has all the water and oxygen in the world, it won't be able to ingest the energy it needs without light.

How much light a plant needs depends on its individual needs. Here is a guide to common light requirements for indoor and outdoor plants.

Indoor Plants

When researching the light requirements for indoor plants, you'll see directives like "bright, indirect light" or "low-light tolerant." While these instructions may be subjective, here are some basic rules of thumb.

Direct Light: This is the most intense light you'll find in an indoor space, usually through southern- or western-facing windows. It gives a plant full access to the sun's rays. Direct light may be a bit much for most plants and may lead to wilting and/ or scorched leaves, but there are exceptions. For instance, certain palms, cacti, and succulents can take the heat.

Bright, Indirect Light: This isn't direct sunlight, but it's not too far off. Eastern-facing windows or a few feet away from southern- or western-facing windows are often great sources of bright, indirect light. Here's a handy trick: If your plant casts a shadow, but the shadow is blurry and indistinct rather than sharp, the plant is probably in bright, indirect light.

Medium Light: This is for areas that are a little farther (maybe a few feet) away from a window—they still receive steady light, but it's indirect.

Low Light: This refers to areas that are even farther away from a window, such as the back of a room or by a window that doesn't let in much light. Usually, northern-facing windows receive the least light. Some plants actually thrive in low light. Others can adapt to or tolerate it. Either way, plants will typically grow more slowly in low light.

WHAT ABOUT ARTIFICIAL LIGHT?

What if you're interested in putting a plant where there's not much natural light? In many cases, artificial light could do the trick. But don't rely on overhead lighting or typical light bulbs, because they don't offer the right type of light for photosynthesis. They often emit green light, which plants can't absorb very well.

Designated "grow lights" typically emit blue or red light, which helps plants convert light to energy so they can perform the vital plant processes that keep them alive and thriving.

Outdoor Plants

Outdoor plants come with a whole different set of light directives than indoor plants. Here are some common ones.

Full Sun: Typically, a full-sun location will receive between six and eight hours of direct sunlight per day, usually during peak daylight hours.

Partial Shade/Partial Sun:

Often, the terms *partial shade* and *partial sun* are used interchangeably. These typically mean four to six hours of sunlight per day, but the sunlight may be earlier in the morning than a full-sun spot.

Full Shade: Don't be misled – this doesn't actually mean no sun. Very few plants can survive in darkness. *Full shade* typically means "filtered/dappled sunlight" (such as under a tree) or about four hours of full sunlight, usually in the morning or late afternoon.

Water

There are plenty of reasons to keep your plants well-hydrated. For one, plants need water for nutrient transfer, or the process of absorbing nutrients from soil. It also helps with transpiration, the process that allows water to move up a plant's stem to deliver moisture from the roots to the leaves. Without this flow of water and nutrients, the

cells of your plant will lose strength and your plant will start to wilt.

But how much water does your plant need, and how often does it need it? Unfortunately, there's no single answer to this question.

Plants have individualized needs. For example, a cactus might only need to be watered every few weeks. A moisture-loving plant might need to

be watered every few days
and might even like having a
humidifier nearby.

A plant's needs may also vary
depending on the season. Just
as you might feel thirstier in the
summer when it's hot outside,
your plants will need more water
at certain times than at others.

The size of the plant and its
container will also play a role in
determining how much water

it needs. Potting soil is sponge-like; in small pots that don't have as much soil, it will dry out faster than in a huge pot with a lot of soil. So even if you have two pothos plants, if they're in different-sized containers, they may need different amounts of water.

Watering Best Practices

- Insert your finger into soil up to the second knuckle to determine dryness. Keep in mind that a lot of plants will benefit from mostly or completely drying out between waterings.

- Use room temperature water. It might be tempting to warm your plant up in winter with some hot

water or cool it down with ice water in the summer. These temperature extremes can shock and potentially damage the plant.

- Don't just water one spot. Water evenly around the plant, saturating the soil without making it a mud bath. As much as possible, try to avoid splashing water on the plant's leaves, as that can create bleached-out-looking spots.

- If your plant is in a container, a general rule of thumb is to water one-quarter to one-third of the container's volume. For containers with a drainage hole, you should see excess water drain out the bottom.

Humidity

Plants prefer to live in conditions that mimic their natural habitat. Many indoor plants are originally from the tropics and crave the humidity of their respective homelands.

This can be problematic if you live in a dry area or if you heat your home in the winter. Here are some quick and easy

tips for creating a more humid atmosphere:

- Keep your plant in a more humid space, such as a bathroom or a kitchen.

- Group plants together—that increases the overall humidity level.

- Place a humidifier near the plant to amp up the moisture level in the air.

Soil

Did you know that not all plants
need soil? For instance, soil can
actually kill air plants. Some
plants can grow in water, no soil
required. But since many plants do
need it, it's worth getting to know.

What Is Soil, Anyway?

Soil is a mélange of things, like organic matter, gases, liquids, minerals, and organisms. It's a place to put your plant, but so much more. It has life-supporting powers, like letting your plant receive and transport water, which is vital for the plant's health and survival.

Some soil types let water drain easily; others hold on to moisture longer. Different types of plants

will thrive in different types of soil, so let's get you up to speed on some of the most common types.

Potting Soil versus Garden Soil

If you go to purchase soil at a garden center, you'll probably see two key types: potting soil and garden soil. Confused? Here's the deal.

Potting Soil: This technically isn't soil at all! It's a mix of different organic materials, such as compost, peat moss, perlite, and more. For many plants, this mixture is actually superior to soil. That's because soil attracts a lot of fungi and pathogens that could potentially kill your plant. Potting soil provides a lot of what you need in terms of drainage and nutrients. So why not use

potting soil for everything? Look at the price tag and you'll see. Potting soil is too expensive to fill an entire garden, so it's typically limited to pots and containers.

Garden Soil: This is enriched topsoil (the topmost layer of soil from the earth). Since an outdoor garden typically doesn't contend with the same drainage issues as potted plants, it's usually suitable

for most outdoor plants that are
planted in the earth.

What about Soil
for Succulents?

Typical potting or gardening
soil doesn't always drain quickly
enough for drought-resistant
plants, like cacti or succulents.
Given the popularity of these
plants, it's usually easy to find

cacti or succulent soil mix at most garden centers. However, it's also possible to make your own. Here's one common "recipe":

- 3 parts potting soil
- 3 parts sand
- 2 parts perlite or pumice

Key Types of Soil

Wanna plant something in your backyard? Take the time to figure out what type of soil you have. This can help you choose the most appropriate plants for your space. Or, it can help you figure out how to enrich your soil to make it more appropriate for what you want to grow.

Chalky Soil: This large-grained soil has a somewhat rocky texture. It usually lies on top of chalk or limestone bedrock. It drains freely but doesn't retain much moisture. It's a highly alkaline soil, which will rule out some types of plant life, though fertilizers can help and steps can be taken to balance the pH. Bulbs, some shrubs, and some vegetables do well in chalky soil.

Clay Soil: With a wet, clumpy texture and a grayish look, it's pretty easy to see why this is called "clay soil." It's great at retaining water but not so great at draining, since the aeration isn't good and often requires drainage assistance to help plants grow. Ornamental trees and shrubs and some perennials thrive in clay soil.

Loamy Soil: This fine-textured soil is made of clay, sand, and silt in roughly equal proportions. It's a study in moderation: It drains well, retains a moderate amount of moisture, and is sufficiently airy to avoid root suffocation. It's a good choice for many perennials, bamboo, shrubs, and numerous types of vegetables.

Peaty Soil: This dark soil feels spongy and moist, thanks to a large amount of peat, which is composed of partially decayed organic matter or vegetation. It can retain a lot of water, so it usually requires drainage. It's a highly acidic soil, which can mean fewer nutrients; compost can be used to lower the acidity. Shrubs such as camellia and some vegetable crops fare well in peaty soil.

Sandy Soil: This is a dry, crumbly, gritty-textured soil with many fine grains of sand. It dries out quickly and drains easily and is generally simple to work with. The bad news? It doesn't hold on to nutrients efficiently. However, provided it's supplemented with some sort of fertilizer, it's a good place to grow bulbs, such as tulips, root crops, and hibiscus.

Silty Soil: This soft soil is rich in silt, a granular material mostly composed of quartz, which allows it to retain a lot of moisture. As long as there's good drainage, this type of soil is great for growing fruits and vegetables, shrubs, and some perennials.

LOCATION, LOCATION, LOCATION! WHERE SHOULD MY PLANT GO?

I f you wanted to move into a new home, you probably wouldn't just settle on any old apartment or house. Your decision would be based

on a mix of your needs and preferences. Plants are the same way. Here are some important things to know when choosing prime real estate for your plant.

Should My Plant Live Inside or Outside (or Both)?

Should your plant live indoors, or should it stay al fresco? That leads to another important question: What's the difference between an indoor and an outdoor plant, anyway?

The biggest difference is temperature tolerance. Technically, all plants started as outdoor plants. But these days, certain plants are considered and even specifically bred as indoor plants, because they have low tolerance for cold temperatures. Taking up residence indoors allows them to live longer and thrive. Be sure to research your plant's hardiness, or ability to withstand

cold—it can help you decide where a plant belongs in your climate. We'll talk about hardiness zones in the next section.

It's also worth noting that some plants can thrive both indoors and outdoors. For example, a lot of plants really enjoy a summer vacation outdoors and can be brought back inside before the first frost. If you'd like to take this approach, keep in mind that transferring a plant from inside to outside can be jarring. Help ease the transition by following these steps:

- To start, put your plant outside in a shady area for a few hours.

- Bring it back in for the night. Incrementally increase the plant's time outdoors over a week or so.

- After about five days, you can let your plant have some morning sun exposure as part of its visit outside. However, avoid letting plants sit in full sun.

In the Zone

Figuring out a plant's hardiness
zone can help you determine
whether a plant should live
indoors or outdoors. It's possible
that when researching or
purchasing a plant, you noticed
that it has a designated hardiness
zone that is expressed as a number.
But what does that mean?

Hardiness refers to how well a plant will fare in cold temperatures. The United States Department of Agriculture (USDA) has a handy little plant hardiness map that divvies up North America into 11 different zones. They're determined by the area's average low temperatures. The lower the zone number, the lower the temperatures. There are more

specific zones within the zones, but that's the main idea.

Knowing your hardiness zone can help you choose the best plants for your climate. For outdoor plants, it can help you understand if the plant will work as an annual or a perennial in your area. Or, it can help you understand if it's a plant that you'll need to move inside or should just keep indoors to begin with.

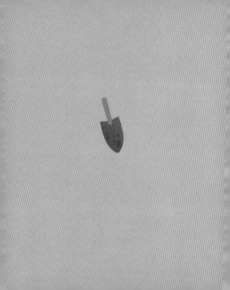

ANNUALS, PERENNIALS, EVERGREENS: WHAT'S THE DIFFERENCE?

Particularly with outdoor plants, there are a variety of different growth cycles. Some plants bloom hard and die young. Others come back yearly.

Others never really go away. Let's talk about some common types.

Annuals: The term *annual* might lead you to believe that these plants come back annually. Nope, tricked ya. They actually only live for one season, so they need to be replanted annually. However, they often reward you for the work of planting by blooming for an extended time period. Petunias,

sunflowers, and zinnias are
popular annuals.

Perennials: Perennial plants are
the type that keep coming back,
and, in the right conditions, they'll
regrow every year. However,
they typically have a shorter
blooming period compared to
annuals. Coneflower and lavender
are popular perennials. *Note:*
Sometimes, a plant can be a

perennial in a warm-weather area but may be considered an annual in areas that have cooler weather in the winter.

Evergreens: These are plants that keep their leaves for more than one growing season. Some examples of evergreens are juniper, boxwood, and rhododendrons.

Biennials: These are less common and follow a two-year biological cycle. They start with seeds that produce the plant's roots, stems, and leaves during the first season. Then, during the second season, the growth comes to completion with the formation of flowers/fruit/seeds. Black-eyed Susans and hollyhocks are examples of biennials.

GROW YOUR OWN WAY: CHOOSING THE BEST PLANT FOR YOU

Now that you've learned some of the basics of plant care and placement, you may be wondering what type of plant is best for you. To further help you

narrow it down, here are some questions to ask yourself.

Where Will You Put It? Consider your living situation and where you'd like to put your plant. Do you live in a tropical climate where you can put a plant outside on a patio or in the earth? Maybe the colorful blooms of a sun-loving hibiscus plant will suit you well. Alternatively, do you live

in an urban apartment, without
much light, where you'll keep your
plant on a windowsill? A plant
that's tolerant of low light, like
the cast-iron plant, might be more
appropriate.

What Appeals to You Visually?

Do you love showy blooms, or do
you prefer simple green foliage?
Do you want a plant that's going
to stay small or one that has the

potential to grow tall? Plants come in all shapes, colors, and sizes. Consider what appeals to you, and research a plant's growth potential before deciding to make it your own.

What Level of Maintenance Can You Commit to? Some

plants require more maintenance than others. So, for instance, if you travel a lot and can only water a plant once every week or so or

if you're prone to forgetfulness,
you should choose plants that
are more self-sufficient and don't
require much care.

Is It an Annual or a Perennial?

If you're planting outdoors,
consider whether you want a plant
that will come back year after year
or one that you'll need to replant
every year.

BLOOM WHERE YOU ARE PLANTED: CONTAINERS, RAISED BEDS, AND OUTDOOR GARDENS

To the uninitiated, it may seem like a mystery: Is it better to put my plant in a container or in the ground?

First, you'll need to determine whether or not your plant is suitable for the indoors or outdoors (see page 51).

For indoor plants, it's a no-brainer: They will clearly need to be in some sort of container.

Planters, hanging baskets, pots—they come in all shapes and sizes.

In general, outdoor plants will grow better in the ground when the soil is appropriate for the type of plant in question (see soil types, page 43). However, there may be exceptions to this rule. Here's a quick guide to some of the common vessels and when to use them.

Container: If your soil isn't conducive to growing the type of plant you'd like, if you don't have a spot that gets enough sun, or if you have a plant that isn't hardy enough to survive the winter and you'd like to move it indoors when the weather gets colder, a container will be the way to go. Drainage holes are key—they will help excess water seep out of the pot after you water. This prevents water

from pooling and protects your plant's roots from rot and bacteria.

Raised Beds: This is a type of container that stays outdoors. It's a frame usually made from wood or another building material. Raised beds vary in size, depending on the materials and your preferences. Gardening in raised beds has plenty of advantages. It gives you better soil control; it

helps avoid foot traffic on plant life; it can improve drainage; and it can discourage weeds. It's also a great option for nontraditional yard spaces, such as a concrete back patio.

Planting in the Earth: This is exactly what it sounds like. If your soil is suitable for what you'd like to plant, this is the easiest way to go. There are plenty of advantages: The start-up costs are lower than raised beds, the earth will generally retain water better, and you can make use of the existing soil.

THE ROOT
OF IT ALL:
MAINTENANCE
FOR PLANTS

Congratulations! You've learned how to tend to a plant's most basic needs. But for optimum plant health, it's worth learning about more nuanced plant needs. Here, we'll talk

about general maintenance tips that can help you keep your plants in tip-top shape.

Deadheading: This is the process of removing spent flower heads from your plant. It's a popular form of pruning. Not only are dying flowers a Debbie downer, but deadheading also keeps the spread of seeds under control and can promote fuller growth of the plant moving forward.

Fertilizing: Fertilizer is a substance that you can add to soil to promote plant health and growth. Fertilizers can be used every few weeks to every few months, depending on the plant. In general, don't fertilize houseplants during winter months.

Propagating: This is the process of breeding your plants to create baby plants. There are several different methods of propagation, depending

on the plant, including rooting the leaf-to-stem cuttings to growing new roots in water. It's a great way to increase the green factor in your home and create gifts for your friends! Some plants with short lives can go on indefinitely if propagated, like string of pearls (see *Indoor Plants*, page 114).

Pruning: This is the practice of cutting away dead or ailing branches or stems. Don't be sad about it—it's just a matter of out with the old, in with the new, and can actually promote healthy growth of the plant.

Repotting: It's not just about aesthetics! Repotting can give plants more room to grow, help refresh nutrient-depleted soil, and generally can give a plant a better growing environment. But repotting can be stressful—it's the plant equivalent of moving from one home to another. So be intentional about repotting, and try not to do it too frequently.

Rotating: You might think that if you found a good sunny spot for your plant, you should leave it there forever and ever. Nope! Most plants will benefit from occasional quarter-turns to help even out the sunlight.

SEEDS OF KNOWLEDGE: COMMON PLANT CONCERNS

Sometimes, bad things happen to good plants. Be prepared! Here we'll address some of the most common plant perils and offer some proactive suggestions for dealing with them.

Overwatering and Underwatering

Plant PSA: Improper watering is one of the leading causes of plant death. Overwatering your plant is kind of like killing it with too much kindness. More is not necessarily better—too much water can cause root rot, which can lead to pathogens that can be a death sentence for plants.

Underwatering is just as bad. A skipped watering here and there may not matter, but frequent neglect can create big problems, depending on the plant. If you're a chronic underwaterer, focus on drought-resistant plants that can withstand long periods of dryness. There's a reason that succulents are so popular.

The Wrong Container

There are two common issues with containers: Either they're the wrong size or they don't have proper drainage. Size matters—a pot that's too small can cramp the plant's roots. Without room for those roots to spread out, the plant's growth can slow down. A pot that's too large isn't the

solution, though. It may hold too much water, and the soil may take too long to dry out, creating a breeding ground for mold, root rot, and diseases.

A lack of drainage is another common issue with containers. Many people replace the plastic growers with decorative pots that don't have a drainage hole in the bottom. Unfortunately, without a hole, water has nowhere to go

and may accumulate, reduce oxygen, and increase the likelihood of root rot. Unless you have a really good understanding of exactly how much water a plant needs, do yourself a favor and always use pots with drainage holes.

Improper Care

Plants are like snowflakes—no
two are alike. While certain tips
will hold true for just about every
plant (like the need for light
and water), the specific needs of
any given plant are variable. By
looking up the specific needs for
the exact plant you have, you'll get
much more tailored advice for its
proper care.

Even if you have a black thumb, some plants are so tolerant that you'll have a hard time killing them. Snake plant, ZZ plant, and many succulents (provided you have plenty of light) are incredibly forgiving of neglect.

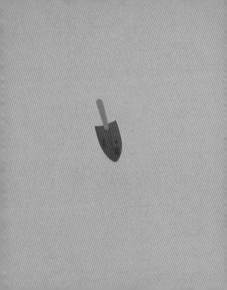

COMMON PLANT PROBLEMS + SOLUTIONS

Not sure what's wrong with your plant? First, look up how to care for your specific plant. Often, growing conditions are the root of the problem. Read carefully and evaluate if you're not meeting one of its care requirements.

For instance, you might have a succulent, and it's in a low-light spot.

Next, look up common problems with the plant in question. It's possible that it's prone to insect damage or disease. This can help you troubleshoot and find a potential solution.

Here's a cheat sheet to common plant problems and potential causes:

Your plant is spindly and not thriving
→ Poor lighting

Your plant isn't growing that fast
→ Poor lighting, damaged root system, overwatering

Your plant is wilting
→ Over- or underwatering, salt accumulation, needs a bigger container

---

Your plant is losing leaves
→ Improper lighting, over- or underwatering, exposure to extreme hot or cold, not enough humidity, insect infestation, disease

Your plant is turning yellow
→ Poor lighting, overwatering, low humidity, insect infestation, disease, not enough fertilizer

Your plant has pale spots
→ Water splashing on leaves, using cold water

Your plant's leaves look burned
→ Too much direct sunlight

Your plant isn't flowering
→ Poor lighting

Your plant's buds are falling off
→ Poor lighting, over- or under-watering, not enough fertilizer

Your plant has mold
→ Fungus in the soil, usually due to high humidity and low airflow

A Quick Note about Pets and Plants

Pets and plants do not always go hand in hand. Even if a plant is pet-safe, your pooch may knock it over, dig it up, or attempt to play with it. Or your kitty may feel compelled to sample the leaves. However, many plants, both indoor and outdoor varieties, are highly toxic to pets. In some cases, the effects are mild.

In other cases, consuming parts of the plant can cause liver or kidney damage, skin irritation, stomach issues, or even lead to death. Be sure to research how pet-friendly a plant is before putting it in your home, or consider putting your plant somewhere that is not accessible to your furry friend.

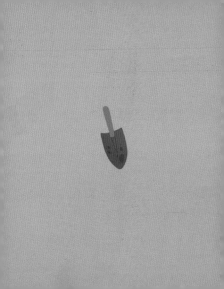

SPECIFIC PLANT CARE TIPS BY TYPE

Certain plant types may require a more specific care regimen. Here's a quick guide to some popular plants with special needs.

BROMELIADS

Bromeliads are unique tropical plants that are prized for their robust rosette-shaped foliage. One of the most famous? The pineapple plant!

Watering: Bromeliads are able to withstand drought, but they can be susceptible to root rot if overwatered. It's extremely important to plant bromeliads in a spot with good drainage.

Humidity: Bromeliads love humidity. This can be tough in the winter, especially if your home is heated with a furnace in the winter. Using a humidifier can help increase the humidity to keep your plants happy.

Light: Bromeliads have different light preferences. Some prefer bright, indirect light and others can thrive in low-light conditions.

However, avoid placing them in direct sunlight for long periods.

CACTI

Light: Your cactus will generally love being in a bright, sunny spot. Most cacti need a minimum of four to six hours of sunlight per day.

Water: Cacti tend to be drought-tolerant. Let your cactus dry completely between waterings,

and make sure you have good drainage. A cactus may need water only every 10 to 14 days.

Soil: Cacti need fast-draining soil. Potting soil won't do the trick. Instead, opt for cactus soil or succulent soil mix (see page 42), which is sandier than potting soil.

FERNS

Light: Many ferns exist under tree canopies in nature, so they generally don't like to be overly dazzled by the sun. If you want to put your fern in a window where it gets a lot of light, keep it a few feet away from the window to protect its leaves. Some ferns even prefer low light.

Water: Ferns are thirsty. They prefer that their soil be kept constantly and evenly moist. If it feels like the soil is drying, it's time to water. But don't water to the point of sogginess—even ferns can be overwatered.

Humidity: Ferns love humidity and need it to thrive. If the fronds are getting brown or you're not seeing growth, mist the leaves or set up a

humidifier. Some people will keep ferns in the bathroom or kitchen to maximize ambient humidity.

IVIES

Light: Ivies like medium and/or bright light. They won't thrive in low light.

Water: Don't overwater your ivy! This can be tricky, since overwatering can make ivy leaves turn brown, which might make you think it's not getting enough water. Nope! Ivy doesn't like wet soil. Wait until the top level of potting soil dries out before watering. A little too dry is better than too wet.

Humidity: Ivy doesn't like very moist soil, but it does like humidity. A humidifier can help keep it moist.

Keep It Cool: Unlike many plants, ivy actually prefers cooler temperatures. Indoors, it will do best in temperatures between 50°F and 70°F.

SUCCULENTS

Light: Succulents love light! They may need six or more hours of sunlight per day. But generally, you'll want to keep them in indirect sunlight. Succulents can actually become scorched in too much direct sunlight. You may be able to gradually introduce them to full sun or put them behind a sheer curtain.

Rotation: Succulents aim themselves toward the sun. If your succulent is static, it's possible that only one side is getting enough light. Give it a quarter-rotation every few weeks, or whenever you water it, to keep things in balance.

Water: Let your succulents dry completely between watering. Overwatering a succulent can kill it. Water succulents by soaking

VINING/ CLIMBING PLANTS

Vining or climbing plants, such as clematis (see *Outdoor Plants*, page 36) or jasmine (see *Indoor Plants*, page 74), can be like wayward children: You need to guide them in the right direction to make sure they don't get into trouble. Here are some simple tips to keep 'em in check.

Direct its growth with some sort of support. To make sure your climbing plant goes in the direction you'd like, give its tendrils something to cling to. This might be a trellis, a system of wires on your fence, or any number of other creative solutions.

Keep its growth in check.
Climbers gone wild! Limiting your plant's growth can ensure that your support doesn't collapse as well as encourage healthy growth. Be sure to pinch off ailing stems or dead leaves regularly.

This book has been bound using handcraft methods and Smyth-sewn to ensure durability.

Written by
Jessie Oleson Moore.

Illustrated by
Lucila Perini.

Designed by
Amanda Richmond.